CHARACTER EDUCATION

I Am Honest

D1712176

by Jenny Fretland VanVoorst

BLASTOFF! READERS

BELLWETHER MEDIA • MINNEAPOLIS, MN

Note to Librarians, Teachers, and Parents:

Blastoff! Readers are carefully developed by literacy experts and combine standards-based content with developmentally appropriate text.

Level 1 provides the most support through repetition of high-frequency words, light text, predictable sentence patterns, and strong visual support.

Level 2 offers early readers a bit more challenge through varied simple sentences, increased text load, and less repetition of high-frequency words.

Level 3 advances early-fluent readers toward fluency through increased text and concept load, less reliance on visuals, longer sentences, and more literary language.

Level 4 builds reading stamina by providing more text per page, increased use of punctuation, greater variation in sentence patterns, and increasingly challenging vocabulary.

Level 5 encourages children to move from "learning to read" to "reading to learn" by providing even more text, varied writing styles, and less familiar topics.

Whichever book is right for your reader, Blastoff! Readers are the perfect books to build confidence and encourage a love of reading that will last a lifetime!

This edition first published in 2019 by Bellwether Media, Inc.

No part of this publication may be reproduced in whole or in part without written permission of the publisher. For information regarding permission, write to Bellwether Media, Inc., Attention: Permissions Department, 6012 Blue Circle Drive, Minnetonka, MN 55343.

Library of Congress Cataloging-in-Publication Data

Title: I Am Honest / by Jenny Fretland VanVoorst.
Description: Minneapolis, MN : Bellwether Media, Inc., 2019. |
  Series: Blastoff! Readers: Character Education | Includes bibliographical references and index.
Identifiers: LCCN 2018033421 (print) | LCCN 2018034230 (ebook) |
  ISBN 9781681036526 (ebook) | ISBN 9781626179271 (hardcover : alk. paper) |
  ISBN 9781618914989 (pbk. : alk. paper)
Subjects: LCSH: Honesty–Juvenile literature.
Classification: LCC BJ1533.H7 (ebook) | LCC BJ1533.H7 F74 2019 (print) | DDC 179/.9–dc23
LC record available at https://lccn.loc.gov/2018033421

Editor: Christina Leaf   Designer: Jeffrey Kollock

Printed in the United States of America, North Mankato, MN

Table of Contents

What Is Honesty?

You broke a bowl.
Mom will be mad.

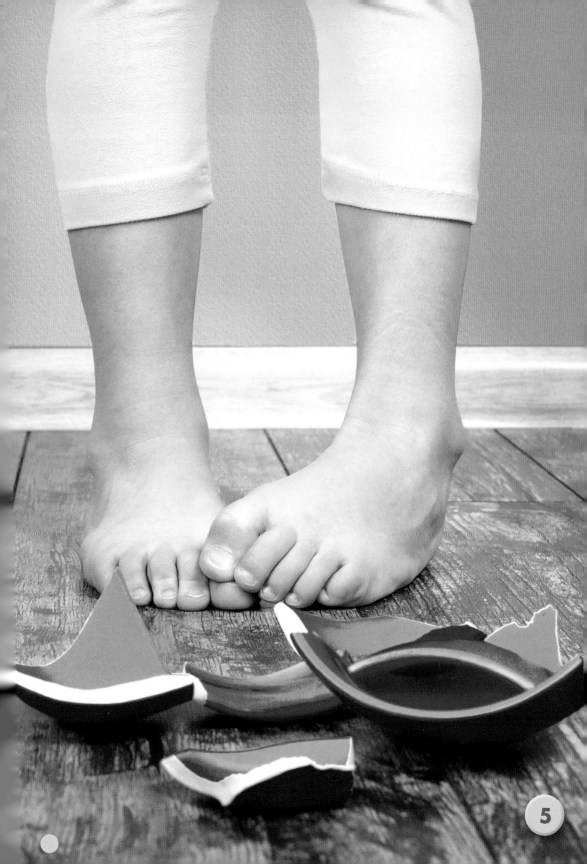

Do you **blame** the cat?
Or are you honest?

Honest people tell the truth. They do not **cheat** or **steal**.

cheating

Why Be Honest?

Honesty builds trust.

It shows you care.

It helps friendships grow.

People want friends who are honest. They know they can believe what you say.

Lies can hurt feelings. People might not believe you when you are truthful.

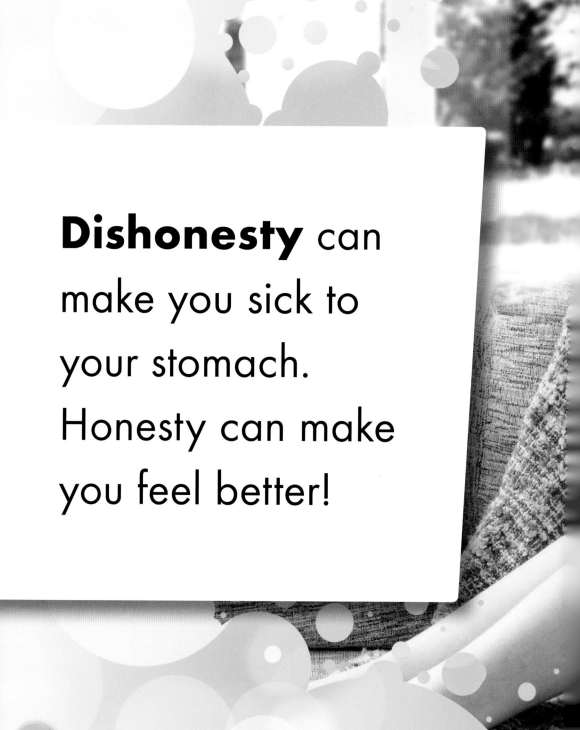

Dishonesty can make you sick to your stomach. Honesty can make you feel better!

Who Is Honest?

You Are Honest!

Be truthful to family and friends. **Admit** when you make a mistake.

It feels good to
be honest!

Glossary

admit

to tell the truth about something that may not have been known

dishonesty

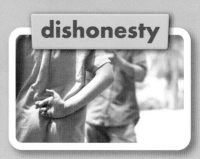

not being truthful

blame

to say someone is responsible for what happened

steal

to take something that belongs to someone else

cheat

to use dishonest ways to win a game or get the right answer

To Learn More

AT THE LIBRARY

Donaghey, Reese. *Telling the Truth*. New York, N.Y.: Gareth Stevens, 2015.

Pettiford, Rebecca. *Being Honest*. Minneapolis, Minn.: Jump!, 2017

Santos, Rita. *Zoom in on Honesty*. New York, N.Y.: Enslow Publishing, 2019.

ON THE WEB

FACTSURFER

Factsurfer.com gives you a safe, fun way to find more information.

1. Go to www.factsurfer.com.

2. Enter "honest" into the search box.

3. Click the "Surf" button and select your book cover to see a list of related web sites.

Index

The images in this book are reproduced through the courtesy of: Stock Rocket, front cover; John T, pp. 2-3, 22-24; Irina Kozorog, pp. 4-5, 6-7; FatCamera, pp. 8-9; Sergey Novikov, pp. 10-11; Distinctive Images, pp. 12-13; kali9, pp. 14-15; Maya Kruchankova, pp. 16-17; martinedoucet, p. 17 (good, bad); LightField Studios, pp. 18-19; Rido, pp. 20-21; michaeljung, p. 22 (top left); Iakov Filimonov, p. 22 (middle left); Zoriana Zaitseva, p. 22 (bottom left); BlurryMe, p. 22 (top right); Maxim Krivonos, p. 22 (middle right).